SCOTT SCHOOL LIBRARY-MEDIA CENTER
Mannheim District No. 83
Franklin Park, Illinois

PROPERTY OF:
MANNHEIM SCHOOL DISTRICT #83
10401 West Grand Avenue
Franklin Park, IL 60131

A ROOKIE READER

I LOVE CATS

By Catherine Matthias

Illustrations by Tom Dunnington

Prepared under the direction of Robert Hillerich, Ph.D.

CHILDRENS PRESS ™

CHICAGO

Library of Congress Cataloging in Publication Data

Matthias, Catherine.
  I love cats.

  (Rookie reader)
  Includes word list.
  Summary: Other animals may be very nice, but cats are the best ones to love.
  [1. Cats—Fiction] I. Dunnington, Tom, ill. II. Title. III. Series.
PZ7.M4347Iad   1983   [E]   83-7215
ISBN 0-516-02041-2

Copyright © 1983 by Regensteiner Publishing Enterprises, Inc.
All rights reserved. Published simultaneously in Canada.
Printed in the United States of America.
16 17 18 19 R 02 01 00 99 98 97 96

I like mice.
I think they're nice.

But I love cats.

5

I like cows.
We could be pals.

But I love cats.

I like dogs,
both short and tall ...

…and puppies and bunnies

...and bears who eat honey.

But I love cats.

I like pigs,
both small and big,
and ducks and geese
and goats and sheep.

I like them all
a great big heap.

But I love cats.

I like birds that sing ...

and bats with wings ...

... and turtles and snails
with shells on their backs.

But I love cats.

23

I like toads and frogs
and polliwogs ...

...and beetles and spiders
and crickets and such.

I like them all very much.

28

BUT I LOVE CATS!

29

WORD LIST

		love	spiders
a	could	mice	such
all	cows	much	tall
and	crickets	nice	that
backs	dogs	on	their
bats	ducks	pals	them
be	eat	pigs	they're
bears	frogs	polliwogs	think
beetles	geese	puppies	toads
big	goats	sheep	turtles
birds	great	shells	very
both	heap	short	we
bunnies	honey	sing	who
but	I	small	wings
cats	like	snails	with

About the Author

Catherine Matthias grew up in a small town in southern New Jersey. As a child, she loved swimming, bicycling, snow, and small animals. *Wind in the Willows* and *The Little House* were her favorite books.

She started writing her own children's stories while teaching pre-school in Philadelphia. *I Love Cats* is her third published book.

Catherine now lives with her family in the Northwest, where her favorite things are gardening, hiking, fog, windy autumn days, and the ocean.

About the Artist

Tom Dunnington divides his time between book illustration and wildlife painting. He has done many books for Childrens Press, as well as working on textbooks, and is a regular contributor to "Highlights for Children." Tom lives in Oak Park, Illinois.